The Anatomy of Goal Scoring in Soccer

Mastering the Secrets to Glory on the Pitch

Dexter E. Hazlewood, MD.

ISBN
978-1-962210-80-5 **Paperback**
978-1-962210-79-9 **Hardback**

Foreword

As a medical student, Division I women's soccer player, and international forward, I have spent countless hours on the field, chasing the ball, dreaming of that moment when the net ripples. Scoring a goal is more than just a physical act; it's a culmination of skill, strategy, and unwavering belief. It's a feeling of pure elation, a rush of adrenaline that courses through your veins.

But scoring isn't just about the game. It's a metaphor for life's challenges and triumphs. Just like in soccer, achieving our goals requires perseverance, dedication, and a willingness to take risks. It's about overcoming obstacles, learning from setbacks, and never giving up on our dreams. In The Anatomy of a Goal Scorer, I'm excited to share my insights and experiences on what it takes to be a successful scorer both on and off the field. From the importance of mental preparation to the art of seizing opportunities, this book will provide you with invaluable tools to help you reach your own goals.

Whether you're a seasoned athlete or simply someone looking to improve your performance in life, I believe this book will inspire and motivate you to strive for greatness. Remember, every goal is a step closer to your dreams. So, let's lace up our boots, step onto the field, and conquer the world.

About the Author

Born in Guyana, South America the author of The Anatomy of Goal Scoring in Soccer has lived a truly international life, filled with diverse cultural and athletic experiences. After spending time in England and then returning to Guyana, the author eventually migrated to the vibrant melting pot of New York. It was here that his most formative years were spent, absorbing the lessons and influences of multicultural interactions that would shape both personal and professional perspectives.

A graduate of Columbia University in the City of New York, with a bachelor's degree in Psychology and concentration in Biology, the author later earned his Medical degree, MD combining the analytical rigor of medicine with the passion for soccer. This lifelong love for the game spans 53 years as a player and coach, bringing a wealth of experience from both on and off the field.

The author holds National Coaching licensure from the United States Soccer Federation and is among the first 18 American coaches to earn a special certification in the La Liga Formation Methodology, conferred in Madrid Spain, a prestigious accomplishment that highlights his commitment to the development of elite players. Currently a coaching consultant to youth teams in Illinois, the author has consulted with teams helping to guide them to great success at both regional and national levels.

Drawing from this unique blend of experiences—as a player, coach, administrator, and physician with a background in psychology—the author has crafted this book to be an insightful and accessible resource. Whether you're a casual soccer observer or an ardent participant at the highest professional levels, The Anatomy of Goal Scoring in Soccer offers valuable perspectives to deepen your understanding of the game and in particular the science and art of consistent goal scoring in the game of soccer.

Contents

Acknowledgments

This book would not have come to life without the support, inspiration, and contributions of several individuals who played vital roles in its development.

First, my heartfelt thanks to my daughter, Cameo Hazlewood, for suggesting and encouraging the authorship of this book. Her assistance with proofreading and her belief in the project gave me the motivation to keep moving forward.

To my son, Hudson Hazlewood, for his continuous encouragement during the writing process and for actively applying the principles of this book on the field. His enthusiasm helped shape the vision for this work.

A special acknowledgment to Coach Kevin LeDoux, a lifelong friend, teammate, and business partner, for providing critical feedback and valuable advice in shaping this book. His encouragement and motivation were pivotal, especially as he prepares to release the complementary companion book focused on defensive principles. His forthcoming work will perfectly complement The Anatomy of Goal Scoring in Soccer, as he delves into the other side of the game.

I also want to express my gratitude to Dmitri Gibbs for paving the way as an author. Dmitri's guidance on the layout design and graphics, along with his encouragement to proceed with this project, was indispensable.

Finally, I want to acknowledge the inspiration provided by two former teammates: Lindon Carter, former youth national player for Guyana, and Patrick Horne, former NASL player. Both have recently become authors of soccer-related books, and their achievements fueled my drive to contribute to the soccer community in a meaningful way.

To each of you, thank you for your unwavering support and inspiration. This book is as much yours as it is mine.

Preface

In the dynamic world of soccer, where chaos reigns and moments define legacies, "The Anatomy of Goal Scoring in Soccer" delves into the heart of what makes the net ripple and crowds roar – goals.

Goals are not just moments; they are the culmination of ten essential attributes seamlessly working together on the pitch: **optimism** that fuels players' relentless pursuit; **technical competence** that turns skill into art; **impeccable timing** that ensures being at the right place at just the right second; **strategic positioning** that outsmarts opponents; **clinical finishing** that leaves no chance for goalkeepers; **mental agility** to adapt instantaneously to unfolding plays; **exploitation of opposition weaknesses** creating opportunities out of thin air; creation of **'chaos'** which disrupts defensive structures; **unwavering trust in teammates** fostering unspoken connections; and **anticipation skills** to decode numbers, predicting movements before they happen.

Each chapter will dissect these attributes, exploring how they interlink and influence one another while providing insights from professional players who have mastered this art form called goal scoring.

Join us on this journey through strategy, psychology, teamwork, individual brilliance – all facets necessary for piercing defenses and achieving glory through goals.

CHAPTER 1: Optimism

In the high-stakes world of soccer, optimism is not merely a fleeting feeling but a foundational attribute that fuels the journey from kickoff to the final whistle. This chapter delves into the essence of optimism, exploring how a positive attitude, confidence, mental toughness, and resilience converge to create a mindset that is unshakable, even in the face of adversity.

The Power of Positive Attitude

A positive attitude is the bedrock of optimism. It is the unwavering belief that success is possible, regardless of the challenges ahead. For a soccer player, this means stepping onto the pitch with the conviction that they will score, not out of arrogance, but from a place of deep-seated belief in their abilities. This mindset transforms potential obstacles into opportunities, allowing players to approach each game with enthusiasm and determination.

"Success is no accident. It is hard work, perseverance, learning, studying, sacrifice and most of all, love of what you are doing or learning to do." – Pelé

Confidence: The Inner Strength

Confidence is the inner strength that propels players to take risks and seize opportunities. It is the assurance that comes from knowing one's skills and the preparation that has gone into honing them. A confident player is not easily intimidated by opponents, teammates, coaches, spectators, or the stakes of the game. Instead, they thrive under pressure, using it as a catalyst to elevate their performance. This self-assuredness is contagious, often inspiring teammates and creating a cohesive unit that believes in its collective potential.

Mental Toughness: The Unyielding Spirit
Mental toughness is the ability to maintain focus and composure under pressure. It is the resilience to bounce back from setbacks and the determination to keep pushing forward, even when the odds seem insurmountable. For a soccer player, mental toughness means staying calm and collected, regardless of the game's intensity. It involves managing emotions, staying disciplined, and maintaining a clear mind to make strategic decisions. This attribute is crucial for overcoming the psychological battles that occur on the pitch, ensuring that players remain steadfast in their pursuit of victory.

"Champions keep playing until they get it right." – Billie Jean King

Resilience: The Ability to Rebound
Resilience is the capacity to recover quickly from difficulties. In soccer, this means not being discouraged by missed opportunities or mistakes. Instead, resilient players learn from their experiences, using them as stepping stones to improve and adapt. This attribute is vital for maintaining a positive outlook, as it reinforces

the belief that setbacks are temporary and can be overcome with perseverance and effort.

Knowing Before the Kickoff

One of the most powerful aspects of optimism is the knowledge that you will score before the game even begins. This is not about arrogance but about a realistic assessment of one's abilities and preparation. Players who possess this mindset approach each game with a sense of purpose and determination. They visualize their success, mentally rehearsing their movements and strategies. This mental preparation instills a sense of calm and confidence, allowing players to perform at their best when it matters most.

Mental Judo: Turning Adversity into Advantage

Mental Judo is a concept that involves using the energy of the opposition to one's advantage. Just as in the martial art of Judo, where an opponent's force is redirected to gain an upper hand, mental Judo in soccer involves turning challenges into opportunities. This requires a high level of mental agility and strategic thinking. Players who master mental Judo can anticipate their opponents' moves, exploit weaknesses, and create scoring opportunities from seemingly disadvantageous situations. This skill is a testament to the power of optimism, as it demonstrates the ability to remain positive and proactive, even in the face of adversity.

"The greatest glory in living lies not in never falling, but in rising every time we fall." – Nelson Mandela

Summary

Optimism in soccer is a multifaceted attribute that encompasses a positive attitude, confidence, mental toughness, and resilience. It is the belief in one's ability to succeed, the inner strength to face challenges head-on, the unyielding spirit to stay focused under pressure, and the capacity to rebound from setbacks. By embracing these elements, players can approach each game with the knowledge that they will score, using mental Judo to turn adversity into advantage. This chapter has explored how these attributes interlink, creating a mindset that is essential for achieving success on the pitch. As we delve deeper into the anatomy of goal scoring, we will uncover more about how these qualities contribute to the art of finding the back of the net.

Unleashing the Power of Optimism in Soccer

Embracing Optimism

Building Confidence

Fostering Resilience

Mental Judo: Turning Adversity into Advantage

Cultivating a Positive Attitude

Developing Mental Toughness

Knowing Before the Kickoff

Summary: The Anatomy of Goal Scoring

CHAPTER 2: Technical Competence

In the intricate dance of soccer, technical competence stands as the cornerstone of a player's ability to influence the game. This chapter delves into the mastery of five fundamental skills—receiving, shooting, passing, dribbling, and shielding—and how combinations of these skills define the type of attacker you are and the threat you pose to the opponent's goal.

Mastery of Fundamentals

Receiving: The ability to control and manipulate the ball upon receiving a pass is crucial. A player who masters this skill can seamlessly transition from defense to attack, maintain possession under pressure, and set up scoring opportunities. Effective receiving involves soft touches, quick adjustments, and an acute awareness of the surrounding space.

"The first touch is everything. It sets up your next move and can make or break a play." – Xavi Hernandez

Shooting: Scoring goals is the ultimate objective, and shooting is the means to that end. Mastery of shooting involves not only power but also precision. Players must prioritize accuracy, knowing when to opt for placement over power. The ability to shoot with both feet, from various angles and distances, makes a player a versatile and unpredictable threat.

"A good striker is not the one who always scores, but the one who always finds the right moment to shoot." – Thierry Henry

Passing: Incisive, high-completion-rate passing is the hallmark of a technically competent player. Effective passing requires vision, timing, and precision. It involves knowing when to play a simple pass to maintain possession and when to execute a more ambitious pass to break through defensive lines. Mastery of passing enables a player to dictate the tempo of the game and create scoring opportunities for teammates.

"Passing is the language of football. It's how we communicate on the pitch." – Andrea Pirlo

Dribbling: The art of dribbling involves more than just speed and agility; it requires guile and the ability to manipulate the ball with ease. A player who excels in dribbling can navigate through tight spaces, evade defenders, and create scoring opportunities. Dribbling with purpose and control makes a player a constant threat, capable of turning the tide of the game in an instant.

"Dribbling is like poetry in motion. It's about expressing yourself with the ball." – Ronaldinho

Shielding: Shielding the ball is essential for maintaining possession and creating space. A player who masters this skill can protect the ball from defenders, hold up play, and strategically involve teammates in the offense. Effective shielding requires strength, balance, and an understanding of body positioning.

"Shielding the ball is about using your body as a shield, protecting the ball like it's your most prized possession." – Didier Drogba

Defining the Type of Attacker

The combination of these fundamentals defines the type of attacker you are and the threat you pose. For instance, a player who excels in receiving and passing is likely to be a playmaker, orchestrating the attack and setting up teammates. A player who combines shooting and dribbling is a direct threat, capable of creating and finishing scoring opportunities. Mastery of shielding and passing makes a player an effective target man, holding up play and bringing others into the attack.

Technical Competence in Action

Prioritization of Accuracy in Shooting: Knowing when to prioritize accuracy over power is crucial. A well-placed shot can be more effective than a powerful one, especially when aiming for corners or exploiting the goalkeeper's weaknesses. Players who master this aspect of shooting can score consistently, even under pressure.

Incisive Passing Distribution: High-completion-rate passing is essential for maintaining possession and creating scoring opportunities. Players must be able to execute both short, simple passes and long, incisive ones. This versatility in passing allows a player to adapt to different game situations and exploit defensive weaknesses.

Guile in Dribbling: The ability to manipulate the ball with ease and deceive defenders is a valuable asset. Players who excel in dribbling can create space for themselves and their teammates, disrupt defensive structures, and generate scoring opportunities. Dribbling with purpose and control makes a player a constant threat.

Shielding to Protect and Hold Up Play: Shielding the ball effectively allows a player to maintain possession under pressure and create space for teammates. This skill is particularly important for target men, who need to hold up play and bring others into the attack. Effective shielding requires strength, balance, and an understanding of body positioning.

Summary

Technical competence in soccer is defined by the mastery of fundamental skills—receiving, shooting, passing, dribbling, and shielding. The combination of these skills determines the type of attacker you are and the threat you pose to the opponent's goal. By prioritizing accuracy in shooting, executing incisive passing, using guile in dribbling, and shielding the ball effectively, players can elevate their game and become formidable attackers. This chapter has explored how these fundamentals interlink, creating a technically competent player capable of influencing the game and achieving success on the pitch. As we continue to delve into the anatomy of goal scoring, we will uncover more about how these qualities contribute to the art of finding the back of the net.

Technical Skills and Attacker Roles in Soccer

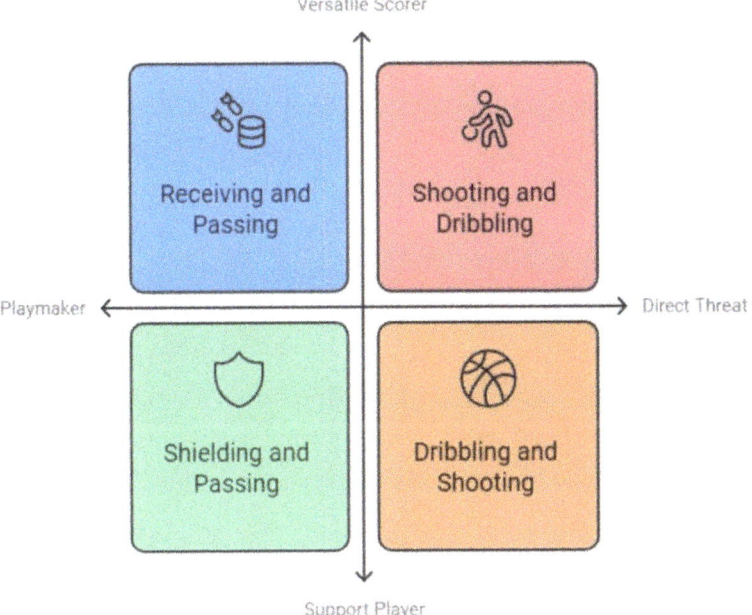

CHAPTER 3: Positioning

In the intricate and fast-paced world of soccer, positioning is a critical element that can make the difference between a missed opportunity and a game-winning goal. This chapter explores the burgeoning science of "scanning" and its correlation with successful goal scoring, emphasizing the importance of disciplined focus, committed offensive support, and anticipatory optimism. We will delve into how awareness, vision, and quickness of decision-making are essential attributes that underpin effective positioning on the pitch.

The Science of Scanning

Scanning, the act of continuously surveying the field, is a burgeoning science that has become integral to elite soccer performance. It involves players constantly moving their heads to gather information about their surroundings, including the positions of teammates, opponents, and open spaces. This practice allows players to make informed decisions quickly, enhancing their ability to find and exploit advantageous positions.

"The best players are always scanning the field, always aware of their surroundings." – Pep Guardiola

Correlation with Successful Goal Scoring: Players who excel at scanning are often more successful in goal scoring. By continuously gathering information, they can anticipate the flow of the game, position themselves optimally, and react swiftly to opportunities. Scanning helps players identify gaps in the defense, predict the movements of opponents, and create space for themselves and their teammates.

Seeking Advantages and Occupation of Space (SSS)
Effective positioning is about seeking advantages and occupying space strategically. This concept, known as **SSS (Seeking, Space, and Scanning)**, is fundamental to creating goal-scoring opportunities.

Seeking Advantages: Players must constantly seek to gain an edge over their opponents. This involves understanding the dynamics of the game, recognizing weaknesses in the opposition, and positioning themselves to exploit these weaknesses. Scanning plays a crucial role in this process, as it provides the necessary information to make strategic decisions.

Occupation of Space: Occupying the right spaces on the field is essential for creating scoring opportunities. Players must understand the importance of spatial awareness and how to use it to their advantage. This involves positioning themselves in areas where they can receive the ball, create passing lanes, and disrupt the defensive structure of the opposition.

"Space is the most important thing in football. You have to be in the right place at the right time."
– Johan Cruyff

Disciplined Focus

One of the greatest challenges in soccer is maintaining disciplined focus. Players often have a natural temptation to follow the ball, but effective positioning requires resisting this urge and maintaining awareness of the entire field.

Advantages of Disciplined Focus: By staying disciplined and focused, players can anticipate the flow of the game and position themselves advantageously. This focus allows them to be in the right place at the right time, ready to capitalize on scoring opportunities. It also helps in maintaining defensive responsibilities, ensuring that the team remains balanced and organized.

"Discipline is the bridge between goals and accomplishment." – Jim Rohn

Committed Offensive Support

Committed offensive support is about being proactive and involved in the attack, even when not in possession of the ball. This requires players to position themselves strategically to support their teammates and create scoring opportunities.

Right Places and Anticipatory Optimism: Players must have the optimism and belief that they will be involved in the play. This anticipatory mindset drives them to position themselves effectively, ready to support the attack. By being in the right places, players can provide passing options, create space, and increase the team's chances of scoring.

"Success is where preparation and opportunity meet." – Bobby Unser

The Role of Awareness, Vision, and Quickness of Decision

Awareness, vision, and *quickness of decision-making* are critical attributes that enhance positioning and goal-scoring potential.

Awareness: Awareness involves understanding the dynamics of the game, recognizing the positions of teammates and opponents, and anticipating the flow of play. Players with high awareness can make better decisions and position themselves more effectively.

Vision: Vision is the ability to see and understand the game beyond the immediate play. It involves recognizing opportunities, predicting movements, and making strategic decisions. Players with excellent vision can create scoring opportunities by delivering precise passes and positioning themselves advantageously.

"Vision is the art of seeing what is invisible to others."
– Jonathan Swift

Quickness of Decision: The ability to make quick decisions is essential in soccer, where the game can change in an instant. Players must process information rapidly and act decisively. Quick decision-making allows players to exploit opportunities, maintain possession, and create scoring chances.

"Speed of decision is the essence of good football."
– Arsène Wenger

Summary

Positioning is a vital component of successful goal scoring in soccer. The science of scanning, combined with disciplined focus, committed offensive support, and anticipatory optimism, enables players to position themselves effectively on the pitch. Awareness, vision, and quickness of decision-making are essential attributes that underpin effective positioning, allowing players to seek advantages, occupy space strategically, and create scoring opportunities. This chapter has explored how these elements interlink, highlighting the importance of positioning in the anatomy of goal scoring. As we continue to delve into the intricacies of soccer, we will uncover more about how these qualities contribute to the art of finding the back of the net.

Key Elements of Effective Positioning in Soccer

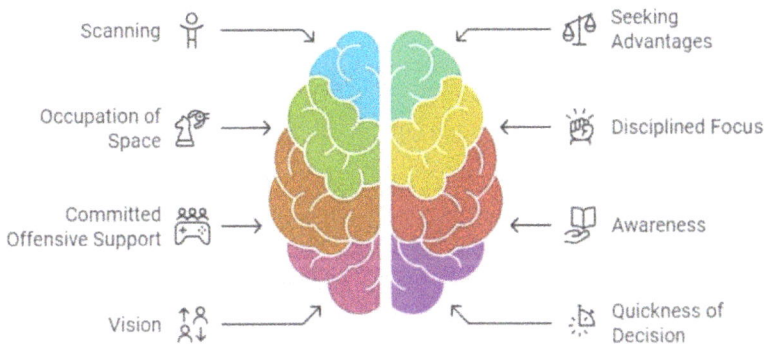

Scanning

Occupation of Space

Committed Offensive Support

Vision

Seeking Advantages

Disciplined Focus

Awareness

Quickness of Decision

CHAPTER 4: Timing

In the art of goal scoring, timing is everything. It is the invisible thread that weaves together movement, trajectory, and arrivals to create opportunities that catch defenders off guard and lead to goals. This chapter delves into the critical importance of timing in successful goal scoring, emphasizing the role of movement, trajectory selection, and coordinated arrivals with teammates. We will explore how these elements combine to make a player the "Visible Ghost"—an "Invisible Thorn" in the side of the defense.

The Role of Movement

Movement is a fundamental aspect of timing. It involves making runs and positioning oneself in ways that exploit moments when defenders are least attentive. This requires a keen sense of awareness and the ability to read the game, anticipating when and where to move to create space and opportunities.

Exploiting Defender Inattention: Defenders are most vulnerable when they are momentarily distracted or focused on the ball. Effective attackers capitalize on these moments, making runs that catch defenders off guard. This could be a sudden sprint into the box, a diagonal run to create space, or a subtle shift in position to lose a marker.

"The best players are always one step ahead, always moving into the right spaces." – Johan Cruyff

Deceptive Movement: Movement should not always be direct. Sometimes, indirect runs can be more effective in camouflaging a player's intent. By making decoy runs or moving in ways that seem non-threatening, attackers can lure defenders out of position, creating gaps that can be exploited.

Selecting the Right Trajectory

The trajectory of a run or pass is crucial in timing. It involves choosing the right path and angle to maximize the chances of success. This requires an understanding of the game's dynamics and the ability to adapt to different situations.

Direct vs. Indirect Trajectories: Sometimes, a direct approach is necessary, such as a straight run towards goal or a direct pass into the box. Other times, an indirect trajectory, such as a looping run or a curved pass, can be more effective in deceiving defenders and creating space. The key is to vary the approach, keeping defenders guessing and unable to predict the next move.

"A good pass is about more than just accuracy; it's about timing and trajectory." – Xavi Hernandez

Camouflaging Intent: By selecting the right trajectory, attackers can disguise their true intentions. This involves making runs that appear to be heading in one direction but then quickly changing course, or delivering passes that seem intended for one player but are actually aimed at another. This element of surprise is essential in breaking down defenses.

Arrivals: Choreographing with Teammates

Effective goal scoring often requires coordinated efforts with teammates. This involves choreographing movements and positioning to ensure that there are adequate and advantageous numbers of offensive players in threatening positions.

Building Numbers in the Box: A key aspect of timing is ensuring that there are at least three attackers in and around the 18-yard box. This creates multiple options for the player with the ball and increases the chances of scoring. By arriving in the box at the right moment, attackers can overwhelm defenders and create confusion.

"Goals are often the result of teamwork and timing, not just individual brilliance." – Lionel Messi

Coordinated Movements: Timing also involves synchronizing movements with teammates. This could be a well-timed run to meet a cross, a coordinated press to win the ball high up the pitch, or a series of quick passes to break through the defense. Effective communication and understanding between players are essential in choreographing these movements.

The "Visible Ghost" and the "Invisible Thorn"

The concept of the "Visible Ghost" and the "Invisible Thorn" encapsulates the essence of timing in goal scoring. It involves being present and active in the game while remaining elusive and difficult for defenders to track.

Movement + Trajectory + Arrivals = Invisible Thorn: By combining well-timed movement, the right trajectory, and coordinated arrivals, attackers can become the "Ghostly Thorn"—a constant, yet elusive threat to the defense. This involves making runs that are difficult to track, selecting trajectories that deceive defenders, and arriving in the box at the perfect moment to capitalize on scoring opportunities.

"The art of scoring is about being in the right place at the right time, and sometimes, being invisible to the defenders." – Thierry Henry

Anticipatory Optimism: A key element of this concept is anticipatory optimism—the belief that the right opportunity will present itself. This mindset drives attackers to position themselves effectively, make intelligent runs, and remain patient, knowing that their moment will come.

Summary

Timing is a critical component of successful goal scoring in soccer. It involves the strategic use of movement, the selection of the right trajectory, and the coordination of arrivals with teammates. By mastering these elements, attackers can become the "Visible Ghost"—an "Invisible Thorn" that constantly threatens the defense. This chapter has explored how timing interlinks with movement, trajectory, and arrivals, highlighting its importance in the anatomy of goal scoring. As we continue to delve into the intricacies of soccer, we will uncover more about how these qualities contribute to the art of finding the back of the net.

Mastering Timing in Goal Scoring

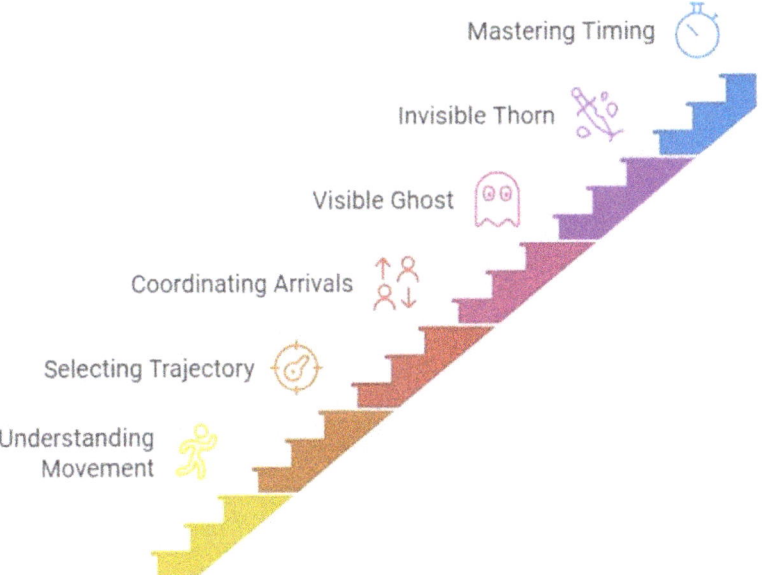

Mastering Timing

Invisible Thorn

Visible Ghost

Coordinating Arrivals

Selecting Trajectory

Understanding Movement

CHAPTER 5: *Fit the "Chaos"*

Soccer is a sport like no other, characterized by its unique blend of structure and unpredictability. It is, in essence, controlled chaos, where a ball can be played in any direction, at any height, and at any speed. This chapter explores the importance of fitting into this chaos to become a successful goal scorer. We will delve into the role of assessing and understanding the rhythm and flow of the game, recognizing prevailing tendencies, and identifying the complementary actions needed to score. By understanding and controlling the chaos, players can increase their chances of finding the back of the net.

The Unique Nature of Soccer's Chaos

Soccer's chaotic nature is what makes it both challenging and exhilarating. Unlike many other sports, the ball can be played 360 degrees, both on the ground and in the air. This creates a dynamic and fluid environment where anything can happen at any moment. Successful players learn to thrive in this chaos, using it to their advantage rather than being overwhelmed by it.

Controlled Chaos: The concept of controlled chaos refers to the ability to navigate and manipulate the unpredictable elements of the game. This involves understanding the ebb and flow of play, recognizing patterns, and making quick decisions that exploit the chaos to create scoring opportunities.

"In football, the worst blindness is only seeing the ball." – Nelson Falcão Rodrigues

Assessing and Understanding the Rhythm and Flow

To fit into the chaos, players must first assess and understand the rhythm and flow of the game. This involves observing how the game is unfolding, recognizing the tempo, and identifying key moments when the game is likely to shift.

Rhythm and Flow: The rhythm of the game refers to the pace at which it is being played, while the flow refers to the movement and direction of play. By understanding these elements, players can anticipate changes and position themselves advantageously.

Prevailing Tendencies: Recognizing the prevailing tendencies of both teams is crucial. This includes understanding whether the game is being dominated by tactics, skill, physicality, or psychological manipulation through trash-talking. By assessing these tendencies, players can adapt their approach to fit the current state of the game.

"The game is 90% mental, the other half is physical." – Yogi Berra

Assessing Impact and Influence

Once the rhythm and flow have been understood, players must assess the impact and influence these tendencies are having on the game. This involves analyzing how different elements are affecting play and identifying opportunities to exploit them.

Impact of Tendencies: Different tendencies can have varying impacts on the game. For example, a highly tactical game may require precise positioning and strategic movement, while a physically intense game may require resilience and strength. By understanding these impacts, players can adjust their approach to maximize their effectiveness.

Influence on the Game: Players must also consider how their actions can influence the game. This involves recognizing moments when they can shift the momentum, create space, or disrupt the opposition's plans. By being proactive and assertive, players can take control of the chaos and turn it to their advantage.

Identifying Complementary Actions

To score goals in the midst of chaos, players must identify the complementary actions needed to capitalize on opportunities. This involves understanding which behaviors and attributes are most effective in the current context and how to execute them.

Complementary Actions: These are actions that align with the prevailing tendencies and enhance the player's ability to score. For example, in a game dominated by skill, quick and precise dribbling may be the key to breaking through the defense. In a game dominated by physicality, strong shielding and hold-up play may be more effective.

Behavioral Adaptation: Players must be adaptable, adjusting their behavior to fit the needs of the game. This includes being aware of which players are performing well, which areas of the field are most active, and how to position themselves to take advantage of these factors.

"Adopt what is useful, reject what is useless, and add what is specifically your own." – Bruce Lee

Understanding and Controlling the Chaos

Understanding and controlling the chaos involves a deep awareness of the game's dynamics and the ability to manipulate them to create scoring opportunities.

Player Awareness: Players must be constantly aware of what is happening on the field. This includes knowing which players are in which positions, what actions they are likely to take, and how to respond effectively. By maintaining a high level of awareness, players can anticipate and react to changes in the game.

Effective Attributes: Different attributes may be more effective in different situations. For example, speed and agility may be crucial in a fast-paced game, while strength and endurance may be more important in a physically demanding match. By understanding which attributes are most effective, players can focus on utilizing them to their advantage.

Behavioral Complementation: Players must bring behaviors and attributes to the game that complement the necessary actions for scoring. This includes being proactive, assertive, and adaptable, as well as maintaining a positive and optimistic mindset. By aligning their behavior with the needs of the game, players can increase their chances of scoring.

Summary

Fitting into the chaos of soccer is a critical component of successful goal scoring. By assessing and understanding the rhythm and flow of the game, recognizing prevailing tendencies, and identifying complementary actions, players can navigate the controlled chaos and create scoring opportunities. Understanding and controlling the chaos involves a deep awareness of the game's dynamics and the ability to manipulate them to one's advantage. This chapter has explored how these elements interlink, highlighting the importance of fitting into the chaos in the anatomy of goal scoring. As we continue to delve into the intricacies of soccer, we will uncover more about how these qualities contribute to the art of finding the back of the net.

Fitting into Soccer's Chaos

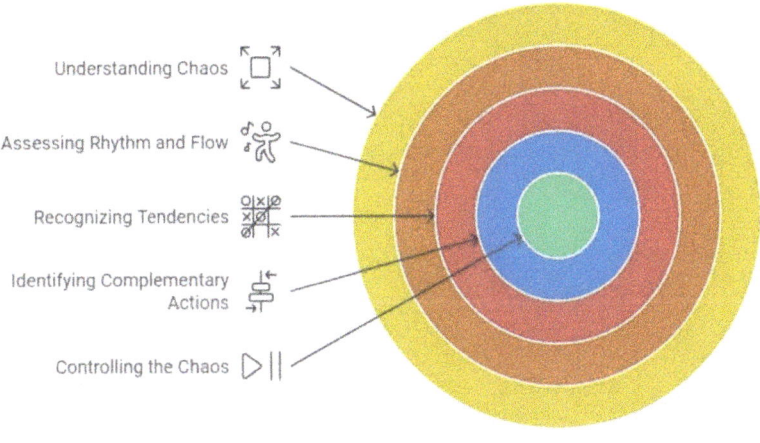

Understanding Chaos

Assessing Rhythm and Flow

Recognizing Tendencies

Identifying Complementary Actions

Controlling the Chaos

CHAPTER 6: Mental Agility

In the high-pressure world of soccer, mental agility is a crucial attribute that separates good players from great ones. It is the ability to think quickly, adapt to changing situations, and maintain a positive mindset despite challenges. This chapter explores the importance of mental agility in successful goal scoring, emphasizing the need to eliminate and insulate against negativity, use dissuasion, cynicism, and criticism as fuel for performance, and maintain belief and expectations.

Eliminate and Insulate Against Negativity

Negativity can be a significant barrier to success. It can come from various sources, including opponents, teammates, coaches, spectators, and even oneself. To be a successful goal scorer, it is essential to eliminate and insulate against negativity.

Recognizing Negativity: The first step in combating negativity is recognizing it. Negativity can manifest as dissuasion, cynicism, and criticism. These negative inputs often stem from others, subconscious fears and insecurities. By understanding this, players can better manage their reactions and maintain focus on their goals.

(*"Negativity often stems from others, subconscious fears and insecurities. By understanding this, players can better manage their reactions and maintain focus on their goals."*)

Eliminating Negativity: Eliminating negativity involves actively rejecting negative thoughts and inputs. This can be achieved through positive self-talk, visualization, and focusing on past successes. By replacing negative thoughts with positive ones, players can maintain a more optimistic outlook.

(*"Positive self-talk, visualization, and focusing on past successes are key strategies. Replace negative thoughts with positive ones to maintain an optimistic outlook."*)

Insulating Against Negativity: Insulating against negativity involves creating a mental barrier that protects against negative influences. One effective strategy is to find a motivational word or short phrase to recite repeatedly. This mantra can serve as a reminder of one's goals and strengths, helping to maintain focus and confidence.

(*"Find a motivational word or short phrase to recite repeatedly. This mantra serves as a reminder of one's goals and strengths, helping to maintain focus and confidence."*)

Using Negativity as Fuel for Performance

While it is important to eliminate and insulate against negativity, it can also be used as a powerful motivator. Dissuasion, cynicism, and criticism can be transformed into fuel for performance.

Dissuasion as Fuel: When others try to dissuade a player from pursuing their goals, it can be used as motivation to prove them wrong. This defiance can drive players to work harder and push their limits, ultimately enhancing their performance.

("When others try to dissuade a player from pursuing their goals, it can be used as motivation to prove them wrong. This defiance drives players to work harder and push their limits.")

Cynicism as Jet Fuel: Cynicism, or the belief that one's efforts will not lead to success, can be particularly demoralizing. However, players can use cynicism as jet fuel, propelling them to exceed expectations and demonstrate their capabilities. By channeling the energy from cynicism into determination, players can achieve remarkable feats.

(*"Cynicism can be particularly demoralizing, but players can use it as jet fuel, propelling them to exceed expectations and demonstrate their capabilities."*)

Criticism as Rocket Fuel: Criticism, whether constructive or not, can be a powerful catalyst for improvement. By viewing criticism as rocket fuel, players can use it to identify areas for growth and strive for excellence. This mindset transforms criticism from a negative force into a tool for development.

(*"Criticism, whether constructive or not, can be a powerful catalyst for improvement. View criticism as rocket fuel to identify areas for growth and strive for excellence."*)

Maintaining Belief and Expectations

Belief and expectations are fundamental to mental agility. They provide the foundation for confidence and resilience, enabling players to perform at their best.

Maintaining Belief: Belief in oneself and one's abilities is crucial for success. This belief must be unwavering, even in the face of setbacks and challenges. Players can cultivate belief through positive affirmations, visualization, and reflecting on past achievements.

"Belief in oneself and one's abilities is crucial for success. This belief must be unwavering, even in the face of setbacks and challenges."

Setting Expectations: Setting high expectations for oneself can drive performance and foster a growth mindset. These expectations should be realistic yet challenging, pushing players to continually improve and strive for excellence.

("Setting high expectations for oneself can drive performance and foster a growth mindset. These expectations should be realistic yet challenging.")

The Role of Mental Agility in Goal Scoring

Mental agility is essential for successful goal scoring. It involves quick thinking, adaptability, and resilience, enabling players to navigate the complexities of the game and seize opportunities.

Quick Thinking: Soccer is a fast-paced game that requires players to make split-second decisions. Mental agility allows players to process information rapidly, anticipate the movements of opponents and teammates, and react accordingly. This quick thinking is crucial for creating and capitalizing on scoring opportunities.

(*"Mental agility allows players to process information rapidly, anticipate movements, and react accordingly. This quick thinking is crucial for creating and capitalizing on scoring opportunities."*)

Adaptability: The ability to adapt to changing situations is a key component of mental agility. Soccer is unpredictable, and players must be able to adjust their strategies and tactics on the fly. This adaptability enables players to exploit weaknesses in the opposition and find creative solutions to challenges.

(*"The ability to adapt to changing situations is a key component of mental agility. Soccer is unpredictable, and players must be able to adjust their strategies and tactics on the fly."*)

Resilience: Resilience is the capacity to recover quickly from setbacks. In soccer, this means maintaining focus and determination, even after missed opportunities or mistakes. Mental agility helps players stay resilient, allowing them to bounce back and continue striving for success.

(*"Resilience is the capacity to recover quickly from setbacks. Mental agility helps players stay resilient, allowing them to bounce back and continue striving for success."*)

Summary

Mental agility is a vital attribute for successful goal scoring in soccer. It involves eliminating and insulating against negativity, using dissuasion, cynicism, and criticism as fuel for performance, and maintaining belief and expectations. By cultivating mental agility, players can enhance their quick thinking, adaptability, and resilience, enabling them to navigate the complexities of the game and seize scoring opportunities. This chapter has explored the importance of mental agility in the anatomy of goal scoring, highlighting how these qualities contribute to the art of finding the back of the net. As we continue to delve into the intricacies of soccer, we will uncover more about how these attributes shape the success of elite players.

Ch. 6 Summary concepts and quotes for quick pregame reference:

Eliminate and Insulate Against Negativity

Recognizing Negativity: *"Negativity often stems from others' subconscious fears and insecurities. By* *understanding this, players can better manage their reactions and maintain focus on their goals."*

Eliminating Negativity: *"Positive self-talk, visualization, and focusing on past successes are key strategies. As legendary coach Vince Lombardi once said, 'Confidence is contagious. So is lack of confidence."*

Insulating Against Negativity: *"Creating a mental barrier against negative influences is crucial. A motivational mantra can serve as a reminder of one's goals and strengths. For instance, Cristiano Ronaldo often repeats, 'I am the best,' to maintain his focus and confidence."*

Using Negativity as Fuel for Performance

Dissuasion as Fuel: "When others try to dissuade a player from pursuing their goals, it can be used as motivation to prove them wrong. Michael Jordan famously said, 'I've failed over and over and over again in my life. And that is why I succeed.'"

Cynicism as Jet Fuel: "Cynicism can be particularly demoralizing, but it can also propel players to exceed expectations. As Muhammad Ali put it, 'I am the greatest. I said that even before I knew I was.'"

Criticism as Rocket Fuel: "Criticism can be a powerful catalyst for improvement. Kobe Bryant once remarked, 'Everything negative – pressure, challenges – is all an opportunity for me to rise.'"

Maintaining Belief and Expectations

Maintaining Belief: "Belief in oneself and one's abilities is crucial for success. This belief must be unwavering, even in the face of setbacks. As Henry Ford said, 'Whether you think you can, or you think you can't – you're right."

Setting Expectations: "Setting high expectations for oneself can drive performance. 'Shoot for the moon. Even if you miss, you'll land among the stars,' is a popular saying that encapsulates this mindset."

The Role of Mental Agility in Goal Scoring

Quick Thinking: "Mental agility allows players to process information rapidly. As Wayne Gretzky famously said, 'I skate to where the puck is going to be, not where it has been.' This quick thinking is crucial for creating and capitalizing on scoring opportunities."

Adaptability: "The ability to adapt to changing situations is key. 'The measure of intelligence is the ability to change,' said Albert Einstein, highlighting the importance of adaptability in soccer."

Resilience: "Resilience means maintaining focus and determination, even after setbacks. 'Success is not final, failure is not fatal: It is the courage to continue that counts,' said Winston Churchill, emphasizing the importance of resilience in sports."

Summary

Mental agility is a vital attribute for successful goal scoring in soccer. By incorporating these quotes and examples, you can paint a vivid picture of how mental agility contributes to the art of finding the back of the net. This chapter will help readers understand the importance of eliminating negativity, using it as fuel, and maintaining belief and expectations to enhance their performance on the field.

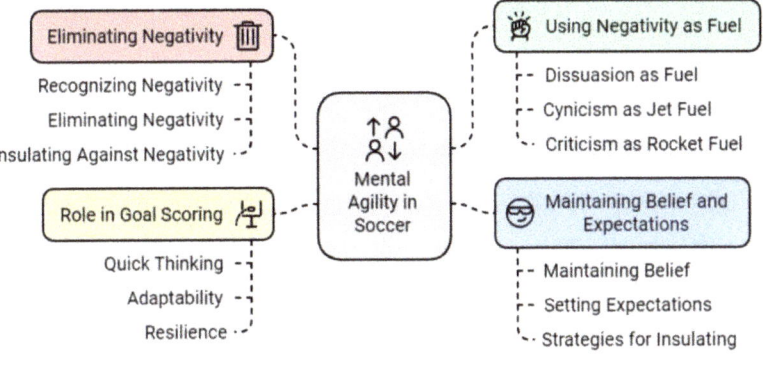

Eliminating Negativity 🗑

Recognizing Negativity
Eliminating Negativity
Insulating Against Negativity

Role in Goal Scoring

Quick Thinking
Adaptability
Resilience

Mental Agility in Soccer

Using Negativity as Fuel

Dissuasion as Fuel
Cynicism as Jet Fuel
Criticism as Rocket Fuel

Maintaining Belief and Expectations

Maintaining Belief
Setting Expectations
Strategies for Insulating

Chapter 7: Exploitation of the Opposition

In the competitive world of soccer, the ability to exploit the opposition is a critical skill that can turn the tide of a match. This chapter delves into the importance of exploiting the opposition, examining how biological strengths, psychological insights, tactical awareness, and strategic planning contribute to successful goal scoring. By understanding and leveraging these elements, players can gain a significant advantage over their opponents.

Biological Strengths

Exploiting the opposition begins with recognizing and utilizing one's biological strengths. These physical attributes can provide a significant edge in various aspects of the game.

Upper Body Strength: Upper body strength is crucial for shielding the ball, winning aerial duels, and maintaining balance under pressure. Players with strong upper bodies can hold off defenders, protect the ball, and create space for themselves and their teammates.

"Strength does not come from physical capacity. It comes from an indomitable will." – Mahatma Gandhi

Core Strength: Core strength is essential for stability, balance, and agility. A strong core allows players to change direction quickly, maintain control of the ball, and execute precise movements. It also helps in absorbing physical challenges from opponents.

Lower Body Strength: Lower body strength is vital for powerful shots, explosive sprints, and robust tackles. Players with strong legs can generate more power in their shots, outpace defenders, and win physical battles on the ground.

"The legs feed the wolf." – Herb Brooks

Foot Speed: Foot speed refers to the quickness of a player's feet, enabling rapid changes in direction and swift ball control. Players with quick feet can maneuver through tight spaces, evade defenders, and maintain possession under pressure.

Innate Physical Speed and Quickness: Speed and quickness are invaluable assets in soccer. Fast players can outrun defenders, create separation, and exploit open spaces. Quickness allows for rapid acceleration and deceleration, making it difficult for opponents to keep up.

"Speed is often confused with insight. When I start running earlier than the others, I appear faster." – Johan Cruyff

Psychological Insights

Psychology plays a crucial role in exploiting the opposition. By understanding and manipulating the mental aspects of the game, players can gain a psychological edge over their opponents.

Identifying Opponents' Zones of Discomfort: Every player has areas of discomfort, whether it's a weakness in their defensive positioning, a lack of confidence under pressure, or a tendency to make mistakes in certain situations. By identifying these zones of discomfort, players can target and exploit them.

Amplifying Discomfort: Once identified, these zones of discomfort can be amplified. This involves applying consistent pressure, forcing opponents into uncomfortable situations, and capitalizing on their weaknesses. For example, if a defender struggles with aerial duels, attackers can focus on delivering high crosses to exploit this weakness.

"The greatest weapon against stress is our ability to choose one thought over another." – William James

Tactical Awareness

Tactical awareness is essential for exploiting the opposition. It involves understanding the strategic aspects of the game and using this knowledge to gain an advantage.

Importance of Tactical Awareness: Tactical awareness allows players to recognize patterns, anticipate movements, and make informed decisions. It involves understanding the roles and responsibilities of each position, the strengths and weaknesses of different formations, and the dynamics of team play.

"Tactics mean doing what you can with what you have." – Saul Alinsky

Respecting the Role of Tactics: Tactics play a crucial role in soccer, dictating how teams approach the game and how players interact on the field. By respecting the importance of tactics, players can better understand their own roles and how to exploit the opposition's tactical weaknesses.

Maximizing Soccer IQ: Developing a high soccer IQ involves studying the game, learning from experience, and constantly seeking to improve tactical understanding. This includes watching matches, analyzing plays, and discussing strategies with coaches and teammates. A high soccer IQ enables players to make smarter decisions and exploit tactical opportunities.

"Football is a game you play with your brain." – Johan Cruyff

Strategic Planning

Strategy is the overarching plan that guides a team's approach to the game. Effective strategic planning involves studying the opponent, analyzing their strengths and weaknesses, and devising a plan to capitalize on these insights.

Studying the Opponent: Thoroughly studying the opponent is essential for effective strategic planning. This involves analyzing their playing style, key players, formations, and tendencies. By understanding the opponent's strengths and weaknesses, players can devise strategies to exploit them.

Analyzing and Capitalizing: Once the opponent has been studied, players can analyze the information to identify opportunities for exploitation. This might involve targeting a weak defender, exploiting gaps in the formation, or capitalizing on a tendency to play high-risk passes.

Neutralizing the Opponent: In addition to exploiting weaknesses, strategic planning also involves neutralizing the opponent's strengths. This might involve marking key players, disrupting their passing lanes, or applying pressure to force mistakes. By neutralizing the opponent's strengths, players can limit their effectiveness and gain an advantage.

"Strategy without tactics is the slowest route to victory. Tactics without strategy is the noise before defeat." – Sun Tzu

Summary

Exploiting the opposition is a multifaceted skill that involves leveraging biological strengths, psychological insights, tactical awareness, and strategic planning. By recognizing and utilizing personal strengths, identifying and amplifying opponents' zones of discomfort, respecting the role of tactics, and devising effective strategies, players can gain a significant advantage on the field. This chapter has explored the importance of exploiting the opposition in the anatomy of goal scoring, highlighting how these elements interlink to create opportunities for success. As we continue to delve into the intricacies of soccer, we will uncover more about how these qualities contribute to the art of finding the back of the net.

Exploiting the Opposition in Soccer

CHAPTER 8: Control the "Chaos"

Soccer is a game of controlled chaos, where the unpredictable nature of the sport can be both a challenge and an opportunity. The ability to control this chaos is a hallmark of successful goal scorers and elite players. This chapter explores the importance of controlling the chaos in soccer, examining how completed plays, advancing plays, encouraging exhortations, and leading by example contribute to this control. We will also delve into how technical competence and the degree of chaos influence decision-making, the balance between advancing the ball and managing threats, the impact of positive feedback, and the varying influences of average, good, and great players.

Completed Plays and Advancing Plays

Completed Plays: In soccer, completed plays are those that achieve their intended outcome, whether it's a successful pass, a well-executed dribble, or a goal. These plays are crucial for maintaining control amidst the chaos. By focusing on completing plays, players can build momentum, maintain possession, and create scoring opportunities. Each completed play contributes to a sense of order and control, reducing the unpredictability of the game.

"Success is the sum of small efforts, repeated day in and day out." – Robert Collier

Advancing Plays: Advancing plays involve moving the ball forward towards the opponent's goal. This requires a balance between aggression and caution. While advancing the ball is essential for creating scoring opportunities, it also increases the risk of losing possession and exposing the team to counterattacks. Players must assess the situation, considering the degree of chaos and their technical competence, to make informed decisions about when and how to advance the ball.

"In the midst of chaos, there is also opportunity." – Sun Tzu

Encouraging Exhortations and Leading by Example

Encouraging Exhortations: Positive communication is a powerful tool for controlling the chaos in soccer. Encouraging exhortations, such as motivating words and supportive gestures, can boost team morale and cohesion. By freely providing positive feedback to teammates, players can foster a positive atmosphere, reduce anxiety, and enhance collective performance. This encouragement helps players stay focused and confident, enabling them to navigate the chaos more effectively.

"You never know when a moment and a few sincere words can have an impact on a life." – Zig Ziglar

Leading by Example: Leadership on the field is crucial for controlling the chaos. Players who lead by example demonstrate composure, determination, and resilience. Their actions set the tone for the team, inspiring others to elevate their performance. By maintaining high standards and consistently performing well, leaders can instill a sense of order and purpose, guiding the team through chaotic moments.

"Earn your leadership every day." – Michael Jordan

Technical Competence and Degree of Chaos

Influence on Decision-Making: Technical competence plays a significant role in how players handle the chaos of soccer. Skilled players can execute complex maneuvers, maintain control under pressure, and adapt to changing situations. The degree of chaos in a game influences decision-making, as players must assess the level of unpredictability and adjust their actions accordingly. For instance, in a highly chaotic game, simple and effective plays may be more successful than risky, elaborate moves.

"Success is no accident. It is hard work, perseverance, learning, studying, sacrifice, and most of all, love of what you are doing." – Pelé

Pass Selection and Success: The selection of passes is influenced by both technical competence and the degree of chaos. In a controlled environment, players can attempt more ambitious passes, relying on their skills to execute them successfully. However, in a chaotic game, simpler, high-percentage passes may be more effective. Understanding the context and adjusting pass selection accordingly can increase the chances of successful completion and maintain control.

"Everything should be made as simple as possible, but not simpler." – Albert Einstein

Balancing Advancement and Threats

Advancing the Ball: Advancing the ball towards the opponent's goal is a fundamental objective in soccer. However, this must be balanced against the increasing threats that come with moving forward. As players advance, they may face more defenders, tighter spaces, and greater pressure. Effective players recognize these threats and adjust their approach, using their technical skills and tactical awareness to navigate the challenges.

"In the midst of chaos, there is also opportunity."
– Sun Tzu

Managing Threats: Managing threats involves recognizing potential risks and taking steps to mitigate them. This could include maintaining possession, choosing safer passes, or positioning teammates to support the play. By balancing advancement with threat management, players can maintain control and create scoring opportunities without exposing their team to unnecessary risks.

"Attack wins you games, defense wins you titles." – Sir Alex Ferguson

The Role of Positive Feedback

Impact on Team Dynamics: Providing positive feedback freely to teammates is essential for controlling the chaos. Positive reinforcement boosts confidence, encourages effort, and fosters a supportive team environment. When players feel valued and supported, they are more likely to perform at their best, contributing to a more cohesive and effective team.

"Individual commitment to a group effort—that is what makes a team work, a company work, a society work, a civilization work." – Vince Lombardi

Building Resilience: Positive feedback also helps build resilience. In the face of setbacks or mistakes, encouraging words can help players stay focused and motivated. This resilience is crucial for navigating the ups and downs of a chaotic game, enabling players to bounce back quickly and maintain their performance.

"The greatest glory in living lies not in never falling, but in rising every time we fall." – Nelson Mandela

The Influence of Average, Good, and Great Players

Average Players: Average players typically hold the line, maintaining a steady presence without significantly influencing the game positively or negatively. While they may not make game-changing plays, their consistency and reliability provide a foundation for the team. They help maintain order and stability, contributing to the overall control of the chaos.

"A football team is like a piano. You need eight men to carry it and three who can play the damn thing."
– Bill Shankly

Good Players: Good players positively impact the game through their skills, decision-making, and contributions. They can create scoring opportunities, make crucial defensive plays, and elevate the team's performance. Good players also inspire confidence in their teammates, helping to control the chaos through their consistent and effective play.

"Talent without working hard is nothing."
– Cristiano Ronaldo

Great Players: Great players do everything that good players do, but they also elevate the players around them. Their presence on the field inspires others to raise their game, creating a ripple effect that enhances the entire team's performance. Great players are often game changers, capable of making decisive plays that turn the tide of a match. Their ability to control the chaos and lead by example makes them invaluable assets to any team.

"You have to fight to reach your dream. You have to sacrifice and work hard for it." – Lionel Messi

Impact Players: Impact players are the ultimate game changers. Their superior performances inspire others to elevate their game, creating a dynamic and motivated team environment. Impact players can single-handedly shift the momentum of a game, making them crucial for controlling the chaos and achieving success.

"When people succeed, it is because of hard work. Luck has nothing to do with success."
– Diego Maradona

Summary

Controlling the chaos in soccer is a multifaceted challenge that requires a combination of completed plays, advancing plays, encouraging exhortations, and leading by example. Technical competence and the degree of chaos influence decision-making, while balancing advancement with threat management is crucial for maintaining control. Positive feedback plays a significant role in fostering a supportive team environment, and the influence of average, good, and great players shapes the team's ability to navigate the chaos. This chapter has explored the importance of controlling the chaos in the anatomy of goal scoring, highlighting how these elements interlink to create opportunities for success. As we continue to delve into the intricacies of soccer, we will uncover more about how these qualities contribute to the art of finding the back of the net.

*Ch. 8 Summary concepts and quotes for quick pregame reference:

Completed Plays and Advancing Plays

Completed Plays: "Every successful pass, dribble, or goal is a building block in the architecture of control.

As legendary coach Johan Cruyff once said, 'Soccer is simple, but it is difficult to play simple.' Each completed play simplifies the chaos, creating a rhythm that the team can build upon."

Advancing Plays: "Advancing the ball is akin to navigating a stormy sea. As former player and coach Arsène Wenger noted, 'The greatest difficulty in soccer is to play simple football.' Players must balance aggression with caution, making split-second decisions that can either propel the team forward or leave them vulnerable."

Encouraging Exhortations and Leading by Example

Encouraging Exhortations: "Positive communication is the glue that holds a team together in the midst of chaos. As motivational speaker Zig Ziglar said, 'You never know when a moment and a few sincere words can have an impact on a life.' Encouraging words can lift spirits and sharpen focus, turning potential chaos into coordinated effort."

Leading by Example: "Leadership on the field is about more than just skill; it's about setting a standard. As Michael Jordan famously stated, 'Earn your leadership every day.' By demonstrating composure and resilience, leaders inspire their teammates to rise above the chaos and perform at their best."

Technical Competence and Degree of Chaos

Influence on Decision-Making: "Technical competence allows players to navigate the unpredictable nature of the game. As soccer legend Pelé said, 'Success is no accident. It is hard work, perseverance, learning, studying, sacrifice, and most of all, love of what you are doing.' Skilled players can adapt to the chaos, making informed decisions that steer the game in their favor."

Pass Selection and Success: "In a chaotic game, simplicity often triumphs. As Albert Einstein put it, 'Everything should be made as simple as possible, but not simpler.' Players must gauge the level of chaos and choose passes that maintain control and momentum."

Balancing Advancement and Threats

Advancing the Ball: "Moving the ball forward is essential, but it comes with risks. As Sun Tzu wrote in 'The Art of War,' 'In the midst of chaos, there is also opportunity.' Players must recognize threats and use their skills to advance strategically, turning potential dangers into scoring chances."

Managing Threats: "Effective threat management is about foresight and positioning. As Sir Alex Ferguson once said, 'Attack wins you games, defense wins you titles.' Balancing offensive moves with defensive awareness ensures that the team remains in control."

The Role of Positive Feedback

Impact on Team Dynamics: "Positive feedback fosters a supportive environment. As Vince Lombardi noted, 'Individual commitment to a group effort—that is what makes a team work, a company work, a society work, a civilization work.' Encouraging teammates builds confidence and cohesion, essential for navigating chaos."

Building Resilience: "Resilience is key in soccer. As Nelson Mandela said, 'The greatest glory in living lies not in never falling, but in rising every time we fall.' Positive reinforcement helps players recover from setbacks and maintain their performance."

The Influence of Average, Good, and Great Players

Average Players: "Average players provide stability. As Bill Shankly remarked, 'A football team is like a piano. You need eight men to carry it and three who can play the damn thing.' Their consistency helps maintain order amidst chaos."

Good Players: "Good players elevate the game. As Cristiano Ronaldo stated, 'Talent without working hard is nothing.' Their skills and decision-making inspire confidence and control."

Great Players: "Great players transform the team. As Lionel Messi said, 'You have to fight to reach your dream. You have to sacrifice and work hard for it.' Their ability to lead and perform under pressure makes them invaluable in controlling chaos."

Impact Players: "Impact players are game changers. As Diego Maradona once noted, 'When people succeed, it is because of hard work. Luck has nothing to do with success.' Their presence can shift the momentum and inspire the entire team."

Balancing Advancement and Threats
- Recognizing Threats
- Mitigating Risks

Positive Feedback
- Boosting Confidence
- Fostering Support

Player Influence
- Average Players
- Good Players
- Great Players
- Impact Players

Completed Plays
- Successful Passes
- Well-Executed Dribbles
- Goals

Encouraging Exhortations
- Motivating Words
- Supportive Gestures

Advancing Plays
- Creating Scoring Opportunities
- Assessing Risks

Controlling Chaos in Soccer

Leading by Example
- Composure
- Determination

Technical Competence
- Executing Complex Maneuvers
- Adapting to Situations

CHAPTER 9: Arrivals in Numbers

In soccer, the concept of "arrivals in numbers" is a critical factor that significantly influences the chances of scoring goals. This chapter delves into the importance of having multiple attacking players in scoring positions, particularly in and around the 18-yard box. We will explore how the number of attackers—whether three, four, five, or more—affects the probability of scoring, both individually and collectively as a team. We will also examine three key considerations: the adequacy of the number of players in attacking positions, the implications of a numerical advantage over defenders, and the impact of the degree of numerical advantage on scoring chances.

The Influence of Attacking Numbers

The presence of multiple attacking players in scoring positions can overwhelm defenses, create confusion, and increase the likelihood of finding the back of the net. The more attackers present, the greater the pressure on the defense, leading to mistakes and openings that can be exploited.

Three Players: Having three attackers in and around the 18-yard box can create a basic level of threat. This setup allows for quick combinations, one-twos, and the ability to stretch the defense horizontally. However, it may not be sufficient to consistently break down well-organized defenses.

Four Players: With four attackers, the threat level increases. This configuration allows for more varied attacking patterns, including overlapping runs, decoy movements, and better coverage of the width and depth of the attacking third. It also provides more options for the player with the ball, increasing the chances of finding a scoring opportunity.

Five Players: Five attackers in scoring positions can significantly disrupt defensive structures. This setup allows for greater fluidity and interchangeability among attackers, making it difficult for defenders to track their movements. It also increases the likelihood of creating numerical overloads in specific areas of the pitch.

Six or More Players: When six or more attackers are present in and around the 18-yard box, the defense is under immense pressure. This scenario can lead to defensive errors, as defenders struggle to mark all the attackers effectively. It also creates multiple passing and shooting options, making it challenging for the goalkeeper to anticipate and react to the play.

"The more players you have in the box, the more chances you have to score. It's simple math."
– Pep Guardiola

Consideration 1: Adequacy of Attacking Numbers

The first consideration is whether the number of attacking players represents an adequate number in scoring positions, creating a high probability of scoring.

Creating High-Probability Scoring Opportunities: An adequate number of attackers ensures that there are enough options to exploit defensive weaknesses. This includes having players positioned to receive crosses, make runs into the box, and take shots from various angles. The presence of multiple attackers also forces defenders to spread out, creating gaps that can be exploited.

Balancing Attack and Defense: While having more attackers increases the chances of scoring, it is essential to maintain a balance between attack and defense. Over committing players to the attack can leave the team vulnerable to counterattacks. Therefore, the number of attackers must be carefully managed to ensure that the team remains defensively solid while maximizing its offensive potential.

"Attack wins you games, defense wins you titles."
– Sir Alex Ferguson

Consideration 2: Numerical Advantage Over Defenders

The second consideration is whether the arrivals number represents a numerical advantage of attacking players over defenders and the implications of that advantage.

Creating Numerical Overloads: A numerical advantage occurs when the number of attackers exceeds the number of defenders in a specific area. This creates numerical overloads, making it difficult for defenders to mark all the attackers effectively. Numerical overloads can lead to defensive errors, as defenders are forced to make quick decisions under pressure.

Implications of Numerical Advantage: The implications of a numerical advantage are significant. It increases the likelihood of creating scoring opportunities, as attackers can combine and exploit gaps in the defense. It also forces defenders to prioritize marking certain players, potentially leaving others unmarked and in advantageous positions.

Psychological Pressure on Defenders: A numerical advantage also exerts psychological pressure on defenders. Knowing that they are outnumbered can lead to anxiety and mistakes. Defenders may become more reactive, focusing on immediate threats rather than maintaining their defensive shape. This can create additional openings for attackers to exploit.

"In football, the worst blindness is only seeing the ball." – Nelson Falcão Rodrigues

Consideration 3: Degree of Numerical Advantage

The third consideration is the degree to which there is a numerical advantage and how it affects the chances of scoring individually and collectively as a team.

Impact of Degree of Advantage: The greater the numerical advantage, the higher the chances of scoring. A slight numerical advantage (e.g., 4 attackers vs. 3 defenders) can create opportunities, but a more significant advantage (e.g., 6 attackers vs. 3 defenders) can overwhelm the defense entirely. The degree of advantage influences the complexity and variety of attacking plays that can be executed.

Individual Scoring Chances: For individual players, a numerical advantage increases the likelihood of receiving the ball in a scoring position. It also provides more space and time to make decisions, improving the quality of shots and passes. Players can take advantage of the confusion and gaps created by the numerical overload to find better scoring opportunities.

Collective Scoring Chances: Collectively, a numerical advantage enhances the team's ability to maintain possession, create passing lanes, and execute coordinated attacks. It allows for more intricate and dynamic attacking patterns, increasing the overall effectiveness of the team's offense. The presence of multiple attackers also means that if one player is marked or blocked, others are available to continue the attack.

"Football is a game of mistakes. Whoever makes the fewest mistakes wins." – Johan Cruyff

Summary

Arrivals in numbers is a crucial concept in the anatomy of goal scoring in soccer. The presence of multiple attacking players in scoring positions significantly influences the chances of scoring, both individually and collectively as a team. By considering the adequacy of attacking numbers, the implications of a numerical advantage, and the impact of the degree of advantage, players and teams can optimize their attacking strategies. This chapter has explored how these considerations interlink, highlighting the importance of arrivals in numbers in creating high-probability scoring opportunities and overwhelming defenses. As we continue to delve into the intricacies of soccer, we will uncover more about how these qualities contribute to the art of finding the back of the net.

Chapter 10: In Teammates, We Trust

In the intricate and dynamic world of soccer, trust among teammates is a cornerstone of successful goal scoring. This chapter delves into the importance of trust in the anatomy of goal scoring, exploring how decisions to give, receive, occupy, and change position are all influenced by the trust players have in one another. We will discuss how building trust is essential, how mistrust manifests in certain playing styles, and the critical role trust plays in the seamless execution of plays on the field.

The Role of Trust in Decision-Making

Trust is fundamental to the decisions players make on the field. Whether it's deciding to pass, receive, occupy space, or change position, trust in teammates influences every action.

Giving the Ball: The decision to pass the ball is heavily influenced by trust. Players must trust that their teammates will be in the right position to receive the ball and have the technical competence to control it, especially in tight situations. This trust allows for quick, fluid passing that can break down defenses and create scoring opportunities.

"Trust is the glue of life. It's the most essential ingredient in effective communication. It's the foundational principle that holds all relationships." – *Stephen Covey*

Receiving the Ball: Trust is equally important when receiving the ball. Players must trust that their teammates will deliver accurate passes and that they will have the support needed to maintain possession. This trust enables players to focus on their next move, whether it's dribbling, passing, or shooting.

Occupying Space: Trust plays a crucial role in positioning. Players must trust that their teammates will cover for them if they move into an attacking position and that they will receive the ball if they find space. This trust allows for dynamic movement and effective use of the field.

Changing Position: The decision to change position, whether through running, adjusting trajectory, or altering pace, is influenced by trust. Players must trust that their teammates will recognize and respond to their movements, creating opportunities for coordinated attacks.

Building Trust Among Teammates

Building trust among teammates is essential for successful goal scoring. Trust fosters cohesion, enhances communication, and enables players to perform at their best.

Communication: Effective communication is the foundation of trust. Players must communicate clearly and consistently, both verbally and non-verbally. This includes calling for the ball, signaling movements, and providing feedback. Clear communication helps build understanding and trust among teammates.

"The single biggest problem in communication is the illusion that it has taken place."
– George Bernard Shaw

Consistency: Consistency in performance and behavior builds trust. Players who consistently perform well, make smart decisions, and support their teammates earn their trust. Consistency also involves maintaining a positive attitude and being reliable in both practice and games.

Support: Supporting teammates, both on and off the field, is crucial for building trust. This includes providing encouragement, helping teammates recover from mistakes, and working together to achieve common goals. A supportive environment fosters trust and enhances team cohesion.

"Coming together is a beginning. Keeping together is progress. Working together is success."
– Henry Ford

Manifestations of Mistrust

Mistrust among teammates can significantly impact playing style and effectiveness. One common manifestation of mistrust is a preference for dribbling over passing.

Dribbling Preferentially: When players or teams prefer to dribble rather than pass, it often indicates a lack of trust in their teammates. They may not trust their teammates to give them the ball back, to be in the right position, or to have the technical competence to receive the ball in tight situations. This mistrust can lead to a more individualistic style of play, reducing the effectiveness of the team as a whole.

Technical Competence: Mistrust can also stem from doubts about teammates' technical abilities. Players may hesitate to pass the ball if they don't trust their teammates to control it, especially under pressure. This lack of trust can disrupt the flow of play and limit scoring opportunities.

Shielding and Occupying Space: Trust is essential for effective shielding and occupying space. Players must trust that their teammates will support them, cover for them, and be in the right position to receive the ball. Without this trust, players may be hesitant to take risks, reducing the team's offensive potential.

Trust Without Eye Contact

One of the most profound manifestations of trust is the ability to play effectively without necessarily making eye contact. This level of trust allows for seamless, intuitive play.

Anticipating Movements: Trust enables players to anticipate their teammates' movements without needing constant visual confirmation. This includes trusting that a teammate will make the right run, with the right trajectory and pace, to be in the right position at the right time. This anticipation allows for quick, fluid play that can catch defenses off guard.

"The best teamwork comes from men who are working independently toward one goal in unison."
– James Cash Penney

Non-Verbal Communication: Trust also enhances non-verbal communication. Players who trust each other can communicate through subtle gestures, body language, and positioning. This non-verbal communication is crucial for maintaining the flow of play and creating scoring opportunities.

The Anatomy of Goal Scoring and Trust

Trust is a critical component of the anatomy of goal scoring. It influences every aspect of play, from decision-making to execution.

Creating Scoring Opportunities: Trust enables players to make quick, confident decisions that create scoring opportunities. Whether it's a well-timed pass, a coordinated run, or a strategic change in position, trust allows for effective execution.

Maintaining Possession: Trust is essential for maintaining possession. Players who trust their teammates are more likely to pass the ball, move into space, and support each other. This cohesion helps maintain control of the game and increases the chances of scoring.

Enhancing Team Performance: Trust enhances overall team performance. Teams that trust each other play more cohesively, communicate more effectively, and support each other more consistently. This trust creates a positive environment that fosters success.

"Trust is the highest form of human motivation. It brings out the very best in people." – Stephen Covey

Conclusion

Trust among teammates is a fundamental aspect of successful goal scoring in soccer. It influences decisions to give, receive, occupy, and change position, and is essential for building cohesion and enhancing performance. Mistrust can manifest in individualistic playing styles, while trust enables seamless, intuitive play. By building trust through communication, consistency, and support, players can create a positive environment that enhances their chances of scoring. This chapter has explored the importance of trust in the anatomy of goal scoring, highlighting how these elements interlink to create opportunities for success.

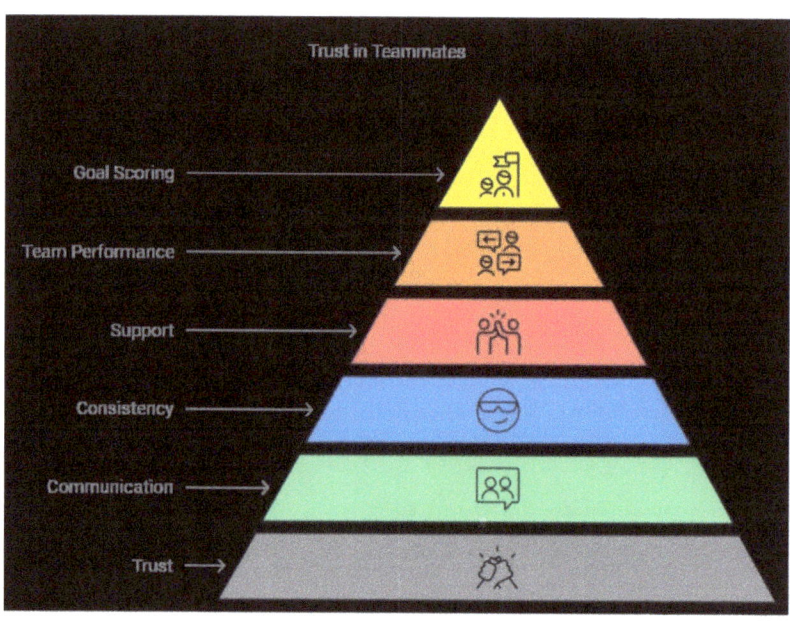

ANNOTATIONS:

- **Pelé:** "Success is no accident. It is hard work, perseverance, learning, studying, sacrifice and most of all, love of what you are doing or learning to do."
  - — *Source: Pelé: The Autobiography* (2006), p. 103.

- **Billie Jean King:** "Champions keep playing until they get it right."
  - — *Source: Pressure Is a Privilege* (2008), p. 12.

- **Nelson Mandela:** "The greatest glory in living lies not in never falling, but in rising every time we fall."
  - — *Source: Long Walk to Freedom* (1995), p. 594.

- **Xavi Hernandez:** "The first touch is everything. It sets up your next move and can make or break a play."
  - — *Source: Interview with The Guardian*, April 10, 2014.

- **Thierry Henry:** "A good striker is not the one who always scores, but the one who always finds the right moment to shoot."
  - — *Source: Interview with Sky Sports*, November 5, 2015.

- **Andrea Pirlo:** "Passing is the language of football. It's how we communicate on the pitch."
  - — *Source: I Think Therefore I Play* (2013), p. 45.

- **Ronaldinho:** "Dribbling is like poetry in motion. It's about expressing yourself with the ball."
  - — *Source: Interview with ESPN*, July 20, 2006.

- **Didier Drogba**: "Shielding the ball is about using your body as a shield, protecting the ball like it's your most prized possession."
  - — *Source: Post-match interview with BBC Sport*, March 22, 2012.

- **Pep Guardiola:** "The best players are always scanning the field, always aware of their surroundings."
  — *Source: Pep Guardiola: The Evolution by Marti Perarnau* (2016), p. 211.

- **Johan Cruyff:** "Space is the most important thing in football. You have to be in the right place at the right time."
  — *Source: My Turn: A Life of Total Football* (2016), p. 79.

- **Jim Rohn:** "Discipline is the bridge between goals and accomplishment."
  — *Source: The Power of Ambition* (1994), p. 42.

- **Bobby Unser:** "Success is where preparation and opportunity meet."
  — *Source: Winning Is Everything* (2003), p. 89.

- **Jonathan Swift:** "Vision is the art of seeing what is invisible to others."
  — *Source: A Tale of a Tub* (1704), p. 37.

- **Arsène Wenger:** "Speed of decision is the essence of good football."
  — *Source: Interview with The Telegraph*, September 20, 2012.

- **Johan Cruyff:** "The best players are always one step ahead, always moving into the right spaces."
  — *Source: My Turn: A Life of Total Football* (2016), p. 81.

- **Xavi Hernandez:** "A good pass is about more than just accuracy; it's about timing and trajectory."
  — *Source: Interview with The Guardian*, April 2014.

- **Lionel Messi**: "Goals are often the result of teamwork and timing, not just individual brilliance."
  — *Source: Soccer Bible interview*, June 2013.

- **Thierry Henry:** "The art of scoring is about being in the right place at the right time, and sometimes, being invisible to the defenders."
  — *Source: Interview with Sky Sports*, 2015.

- **Nelson Falcão Rodrigues:** "In football, the worst blindness is only seeing the ball."
  - *— Source: O Berro Impresso* (1986), p. 72.

- **Yogi Berra:** "The game is 90% mental, the other half is physical."
  - *— Source: Yogi: It Ain't Over* (1989), p. 99.

- **Bruce Lee:** "Adopt what is useful, reject what is useless, and add what is specifically your own."
  - *— Source: Bruce Lee: Artist of Life* (1999), p. 103.

- **Mahatma Gandhi:** "Strength does not come from physical capacity. It comes from an indomitable will."
  - *— Source: The Collected Works of Mahatma Gandhi* (1958), Vol. 58, p. 18.

- **Herb Brooks:** "The legs feed the wolf."
  - *— Source: Miracle on Ice* (1980), documentary.

- **Johan Cruyff:** "Speed is often confused with insight. When I start running earlier than the others, I appear faster."
  - *— Source: My Turn: A Life of Total Football* (2016), p. 93.

- **William James:** "The greatest weapon against stress is our ability to choose one thought over another."
  - *— Source: The Principles of Psychology* (1890), p. 290.

- **Saul Alinsky**: "Tactics mean doing what you can with what you have."
  - *— Source: Rules for Radicals* (1971), p. 122.

- **Johan Cruyff:** "Football is a game you play with your brain."
  - *— Source: Johan Cruyff: The Total Voetbal* (1997), p. 118.

- **Sun Tzu:** "Strategy without tactics is the slowest route to victory. Tactics without strategy is the noise before defeat."
  - *— Source: The Art of War (5th century BCE), Chapter 1.*

- **Robert Collier:** "Success is the sum of small efforts, repeated day in and day out."
  - *Source: The Secret of the Ages* (1926), p. 134.

- **Sun Tzu:** "In the midst of chaos, there is also opportunity."
  - *Source: The Art of War* (5th century BCE), Chapter 5.

- **Zig Ziglar**: "You never know when a moment and a few sincere words can have an impact on a life."
  - *Source: Zig Ziglar's Little Book of Big Quotes* (1997), p. 14.

- **Michael Jordan:** "Earn your leadership every day."
  - *Source: Michael Jordan: The Life* (2014), p. 307.

- **Pelé:** "Success is no accident. It is hard work, perseverance, learning, studying, sacrifice, and most of all, love of what you are doing."
  - *Source: Pelé: The Autobiography* (2006), p. 103.

- **Albert Einstein:** "Everything should be made as simple as possible, but not simpler."
  - *Source: Einstein: His Life and Universe* (2007), p. 473.

- **Sun Tzu:** "In the midst of chaos, there is also opportunity."
  - *Source: The Art of War (5th century* BCE), Chapter 5.

- **Sir Alex Ferguson:** "Attack wins you games, defense wins you titles."
  - *Source: Interview with The Guardian*, May 2013.

- **Vince Lombardi:** "Individual commitment to a group effort—that is what makes a team work, a company work, a society work, a civilization work."
  - *Source: What It Takes to Be Number One* (2003), p. 16.

- **Stephen Covey:** "Trust is the highest form of human motivation. It brings out the very best in people."
  - *Source: The 7 Habits of Highly Effective People* (1989), p. 231.

- **Bill Shankly:** "A football team is like a piano. You need eight men to carry it and three who can play the damn thing."
  - *— Source: Shankly: The Biography (2009), p. 85.*

- **Cristiano Ronaldo:** "Talent without working hard is nothing."
  - *— Source: Interview with France Football, December 2014.*

- **Lionel Messi:** "You have to fight to reach your dream. You have to sacrifice and work hard for it."
  - *— Source: FourFourTwo interview, January 2013.*

- **Diego Maradona:** "When people succeed, it is because of hard work. Luck has nothing to do with success."
  - *— Source: Maradona: The Autobiography (2005), p. 218.*

- **Pep Guardiola:** "The more players you have in the box, the more chances you have to score. It's simple math."
  - *— Source: Pep Guardiola: Another Way of Winning (2012), p. 207.*

- **Sir Alex Ferguson:** "Attack wins you games, defense wins you titles."
  - *— Source: Interview with The Guardian, May 2013.*

- **Nelson Falcão Rodrigues:** "In football, the worst blindness is only seeing the ball."
  - *— Source: O Berro Impresso (1986), p. 72.*

- **Johan Cruyff:** "Football is a game of mistakes. Whoever makes the fewest mistakes wins."
  - *— Source: My Turn: A Life of Total Football (2016), p. 91.*

- **Stephen Covey:** "Trust is the glue of life. It's the most essential ingredient in effective communication. It's the foundational principle that holds all relationships."
  - *— Source: The 7 Habits of Highly Effective People (1989), p. 205.*

- **George Bernard Shaw:** "The single biggest problem in communication is the illusion that it has taken place."
    - *Source: Back to Methuselah* (1921), Part 1.

- **Henry Ford:** "Coming together is a beginning. Keeping together is progress. Working together is success."
    - *Source: Ford Motor Company Historical Archives*, 1922.

- **James Cash Penney:** "The best teamwork comes from men who are working independently toward one goal in unison."
    - *Source: J.C. Penney: The Man, The Store, and American Agriculture* (1973), p. 67.

www.ingramcontent.com/pod-product-compliance
Lightning Source LLC
Chambersburg PA
CBHW051230120626
46547CB00013B/1592